of The Heart and Mind

of The Heart and Mind

Daniel Snell

Copyright © 2016 by Daniel Snell. All rights reserved. This book or any portion thereof may not be reproduced or used in any manner whatsoever without the express written permission of Daniel Snell except for the use of brief quotations in a book review.

Printed in the United States of America

First Printing, 2017

ISBN-13: 978-1-942022-84-8

ISBN10: 1942022840

Iris M Williams

The Butterfly Typeface Publishing
PO BOX 56193
Little Rock Arkansas 72215

Dedication

To every lover around the world ...

> "Love is beautiful and depressing"
> -Daniel Snell

Table of Contents

Wish	20
Shelf	21
Face	22
Crying	23
Strength	24
Beautiful	25
Thankful	26
Streets	27
Blessing	28
Things	29
Dust	30
Karma	31
Forever	32
G-O-D	34
Truth	35
Why	36
If I Could	37
"Lover, Lover"	38
Presence	39
Hood	40
Brutality	41
Thank You	42
My Unborn Child	43

Mom	44
Momma	45
Senses	46
Sex	47
Old Man	48
Memories	49
Talk With The Dead	50
Sun Dance	51
The Good Die Young	52
Picture Perfect	53
Confessions	54
Love	55
Lost	56
This Place	57
Never Say Never	58
Beauty	59
Rainy Days and Rainy Nights	60
Be You	61
Believe	62
Aspects	63
Hoop Dreams	64
Street Dreams	65
Lonely	66
Living To Die	67

Old	68
We Want …	69
Choices	70
Control	71
Life	72
Decisions	73
Grow	74
Signs	75
Friend	76
I Want You	77
Problem	78
You	79
The One I Love	80
Pooh	81
Life	82
Still	83
The Same	86
Head Over Heels	87
My Anchor	88
Imbalances	89
Doing What You Do	90
If You're Not Careful	91
If You Were My Girl	92
No Chance	93

Hard Hearts	94
Difference	95
Voices	96
No Longer	97
Voids	98
You	99
Trill	100
History	101
Breeds	102
Covenant	103
New Life	104
Make Me Crazy	105
Reality	106
Dissection	107
Fear	108
Taste	109
"2 Heads Is Better Than 1"	112
I Believe I Can Fly	113
Let's Be Real	114
You're My Anchor	115
The Life Sentence	116
Crying Nights	117
If You're Not Careful	118
If You Were My Girl	119

Time	120
The Greatest Love	121
Scared of Trust	122
Can I know Yo Name	123
It's You	124
Alone	125
For You	126
Is Love Truly Real	127
My Deepest Thoughts	128
That Girl	129
Where Can I Find True Love?	130
Move	131
Dreams	132
Inferno	133
Crumbs	134
Wondering	135
Eyes	137
Smile	138
Begin	139
Demise	140
Demise Too	141
Failure	142
A Word from the Author	143

Foreword

There are layers to my heart and mind
So many has been revealed over time
I wish I could share them all with you
To give you all of me is what you want me to do
But how can I give you all of me
When we know there's things you don't want to see
I could open my heart to the world
My pleasures and pain I would quickly hurl
Hiding nothing and revealing the livid
My significant moments showing extremely vivid
Times I had with countless others
Consuming you to the point you smother
It's your choice of what you want
Some will be lonely and others will haunt
I can only be me and give you quality
So, take hold of the parts that you want to keep selfishly
I'm far from achieving mastery
I'm just offering you a part of me naturally

-Daniel Snell

Author Acknowledgments

I want to thank God for allowing me to experience so much in life. I could have died a million times, but here I am sharing this with the world.

Thanks to my loving mother Michelle, my aunts Iris and Kathleen, my sister Shavette, and my brothers; Phillip, Jonathan, Marcus and Benjamin for always encouraging and supporting me.

Thank you to those that I 'forgot' to mention.

I love you all sincerely!

Layer 1

Wish

You are sweeter than cherry pie
Like our current war, for you I'd die
Your face is prettier than a painters most elegant picture
Like Sherbet's ice cream metropolitan, you're a perfect mixture
Your voice is sweet like honey and a humming bird
Like a mountain climber I hang on to your every word
You're smarter than a genius even Bill Gates
Like someone on a bus stop, greatness awaits
You are my every thought
Like a missing person, for you I sought
Your pretty white smith is brighter than light
Being with you just feels so right
You're perfect to me, even though nobody is flaws and all
You'd be my number one wish

Shelf

There's nobody that I truly want in my life
No family, kids and surely no wife
I trust nobody, including myself
Nothing is important to me, not even health or wealth
I'm not suicidal, so my time here is wasted daily
Times of happiness for me is rarely
I feel much better being away from everyone and alone
I don't want to be strong or well known
Being miserable is my comfort zone
So being unhappy never feels wrong
I would rather listen, than talk to anyone
Poking hole in people's lies seems like more fun
Everyone in society seems to be fake to me
There's only fake love and real hate
I will be selfish and be to myself
Should I be kind and put my sincere feelings
On a shelf?

Face

Awaking to your sleeping beautiful face
Feeling the warmth of your body from our overnight embrace
Happy to be laying in this soft bed with you
Maybe I'm a painter that's painting my fantasy come true
Loving the touch from your skin
Hoping this feeling will never end
Amazed about the kiss from your sweet soft lips
Thinking of never letting go of your nice sexy hips
Running my fingers through your soft, healthy, shiny hair
Believing that we make the perfect pair
Looing deep into your beautiful loving eyes
Hoping that you will always be mine
Smelling the sweet scent of your perfume
Causes your overall beauty to loom
Hearing your moan and the soft words from your voice
Persuades me, that I've made the perfect choice
I'm happy everyday
To awake to your beautiful face

Crying

Crying endlessly through these dark lonely nights
The pain is deeper than the ocean floor and out of sight
How can I help myself through this agony?
Should I accept the helping hands of my friends and family?
It's stressful because I long to be isolated
Opening up my heart and mind to others makes me feel violated
The tears ride my face like a surfer does a wave
Relishing this turmoil because it's what I crave
Instead of reaching for help I'll soak in this
Because even though it hurts I still feel bliss
Give me a bottle of cognac and a dark room with no lights
And I'll enjoy every thought
Crying endlessly through these dark lonely nights

Strength

Look in the mirror and examine yourself closely
What do you like about yourself mostly?
Who are you?
Find out who you truly are and stay true
Why are you here?
Figure it out but never fear
Pay attention to what and how your life is now
Is this the way that you ultimately want it?
or do you want to turn it around?
Follow your dreams and follow your heart
Don't give up, this is the time for your new start
Be who you're supposed to be and do what you're supposed to do
Leave your mark on the earth so everyone will know you
Work hard and always finish what you start
Educate yourself as much as possible but
Never lose your heart
Love hard and love always
Build and create whatever but strengthen your family

Beautiful

I'm imagining that death could be a beautiful thing
Because it could stop all of life's pain, hurt and sting
The beauty of life is to live happy and free
It could be with someone else or just me
Life should be taken care of like a newborn baby
Life should be seasoned and taste warm and flavorful like gravy
 No matter how much time has passed, you make my heart sing
I'm imagining life with you could be a beautiful thing

Thankful

I was given life
and now I'm awaiting death
Enjoying the bright days and dark nights
Wondering how much time do I have left
I was given life
It could be sweet as fruit that's ripe
And now I'm awaiting death
But I'm relishing every sing breath
I was given life
Who's to say if I live it wrong or right
And now I'm awaiting death
Debating if I should clean up my filthy mess
I was given life
And I've always wondered why
What am I here to do before I die
And now I'm awaiting death
Wondering how it will happen so I sleep less
I was given life
Even though, I never asked to be here
I'm thankful for every day and night

Streets

The streets can be deceiving
That's why most of the young is leaving
The streets are full of lies and truly cold
Everything is sold and bodies are a toll
People ask, why the good die young
It's because the streets are like a spider's web, always hung
There's more and more informants
People who valued a code are now dormant
Long term, you can't' retire with a pension
You're likely to be dear or in prison or with some tension
The streets hurt you more than help
Think about preserving yourself, health and wealth
The streets will take your life
So, stay in school and do what's right
Don't put yourself in the belly of the beast
You'll regret it for being in the streets

Blessing

My heart is bleeding
So much, I can't' breathe
The air tastes so stale
That I hardly open my mouth
I'm staring at you
Through my watering eyes
All of your lies
And all of my cries
I'm numb all over
And can't feel a thing
My mind is racing
To find what this means
How could you?
Why would you?
Please, go away
I want my healing
To start today
I'm drowning in hurt
But I'll love again
Once my heart can fully mend
Thank you for the lesson
Yes, I'm grieving
But you have been a blessing
I still love you!

Things

The things I want to do
I want to do with someone true
I want to go to France
To learn and enjoy true romance
I want to walk on a warm beach
Drinking ice cold lemonade eating a peach
I want to hold your hand
And walk through the park
Hoping forty years from now
It still feels like our start
I want to create
So many memories and stories to tell
Also, how you capture me
With your spell binding smell
There's so much that I want to do
But I only want
To do them with you

Dust

From dust to dust
That's our life story
But who can truly
Explain the after for me
Everything, man and beast
Is said to come from the ground
When we die, we go back
Is that sound?
I guess it's full circle
But what's after that?
Everyone wonders about the after math
Since no one knows
We can only enjoy life
Staying clear and doing what's right
There's man scenarios, heaven and hell
Suffering and mirth
Mankind goes up and the beast down to earth
Maybe nothing happens
Who knows
Just try your best
To limit your woes
Believe whatever you must
We come from
And go back to the dust

Karma

Miss sexy Darinda
I want to make you tremor
Darinda, Darinda
There's so much my mind will remember
My heart is yours Darinda
And it's forever, not a lender
Simple Darinda
Can sometimes be an enigma
Busy Darinda
Please keep me on your daily agenda
When I'm hungry Darinda
Be my alfalfa
You're addictive Darinda
The best bacteria
Lovely Darinda
I want you all in my camera
You're special Darinda
And I want all of your data
I want you naked Darinda
So, the entire night you're my gala
Darinda, Darinda
You are my sweet Karma

Forever

I love you Darinda!
To you, my heart is forever under surrender
I love and miss your full juicy lips
And I'm in need of a fix
I understand R. Kelly's homie, lover, friend
And hope to have that with you until the end
I need you more than anything
And you were supposed to be wearing my ring
I miss holding your warm brown body
Our cushion kisses leading us to be naughty
Reminiscing that cold winter night
Listening to Al Green's "For the Good Times" was alright!
I took you for granted when we were young
Even though I can't hold or carry a note
For you, my heart sung
I love you from your head to all ten of your toes
I love you to your soul even if you don't know
Like Jodeci "Forever My Lady"
You're my lady and was supposed to have my baby
No matter who we're with or may be
It will always be me and D.D.
In many ways, you're splendor
I love you forever Darinda

Layer 2

G-O-D

I came into this world
Because you wanted me to
You protected me
Even when I didn't know
You spoke to me
Even when I didn't know
I can feel your presence
No matter where I am
Or what I'm doing
Your name is so powerful
Some dare not speak it
But you're loving, kind and merciful
So, people should embrace you
Instead of running away
Thank you, for everything you're doing or will do
And have already done
Allow me to be a blessing to others
And allow others to be a blessing to me
We are nothing without you
G-O-D

Truth

Let me be your heart
Let me be your life
There's so much I want
Besides you being my wife
Let me have your soul
The thing that's most precious
Put it in my hand
Let me see your smile
It's more beautiful than a perfect painting
Let me feel your warm soft hug
That gives me a sense of love and security
Let me enjoy every moment with you
It seems the world is in slow motion
So, beautiful to me
Let me have your heart
Let me have all of you
I promise to always be faithful and true

Why

I am wondering why
Why things are the way they are
Why is life so hard;
Or is it?
Am I defeating myself?
Instead of treating myself
I am wondering
Wondering why things are so simple
But yet so complicated
Why can't I plateau on happiness for the rest?
Of my life
Why?
Tell me why if you know
Or show me the road
So I can see for myself
I am wondering why
Why do I feel lost?
But I feel superior
I'm going but I'm at a stand still
Why do people want me to believe the unknown?
I am wondering why
Why
Why
Why

If I Could

If I could compare you to the wind
You blew my mind the moment you stepped in
If I could compare you to the sun
You brightened my life saying I'm the one
If I could compare you to the rain
You're crying because of the pain
If I could compare you to the snow
You're cold and falling because you're feeling low
If I could compare you to my favorite food
I love tasting you because you put me in the mood
If I could compare you to my dream house
I would be in awe with no words leaving my mouth
If I could compare you to anyone or anything
It wouldn't compare because you're above it all
So I would be settling
How unfair to your vanity air
Compare you, I wouldn't even dare

"Lover, Lover"

Lover, lover where have you gone
I think of you often
Even more when I hear our song
What can I do to find you?

Lover, lover so sweet and nice
You were so warm
But now you're cold as ice
What did I do?

Lover, lover so beautiful and smart
I love you more than anything
Like a shattered glass, you broke my heart
Can we fix it?

Lover, lover I will never give up on you
You give me signs of hope
So I see a journey for us that's new
How long will this be?

Lover, lover I will never hurt you again
I love you deeply
And will be your husband
and best friend

Lover, lover I want no other
Like gravy over biscuits
It's only you that I want to smother
I love you forever, lover, lover

DANIEL SNELL

Presence

I'm thinking of you on this cold snowy night
Listening to music by the fireplace sipping cold wine that's white

Wishing you were here so our warm bodies could touch
We could talk about every subject with no pressure to rush

I would love to rub your soft hands and play in your hair
Eye each other with wonder and enjoy the moments of a silent stare

I would love to hold you until you fell asleep
Rest my head on you so I can hear your heartbeat

When you awake, I would greet you with a kiss
To enjoy your presence day in and out I could only wish

Hood

The hood is deep
And yes, it's dark
With all of the danger
It still has a heart
But it's only for those that deserve it
If you're questioning yourself
Then you're not worth it
Some are crippled, some in prison, some are dead
These are the endings
So don't be misled
Some survive but there are very few
Ask the elders
And listen closely to what they say of the one's
They knew
There's a way through the maze
Be patient but most of all be brave
Do what's right and follow your heart
So you can give your little one's a better start
Be you and do some good
Make it out but still help the hood.

Brutality

Police all over the world are *stealin* and *killin*
What can we do besides *screamin* our *feelins*
It's getting worse and worse
And they get off being a justified perp
The problem is clear
So what's the solution?
All of the arguing and *yellin* in pollution
Sit down and think of a plan
Step by step
This will help take their foot off our neck
If you're black
You may as well face it
You're being profiled on a daily basis
Love your skin but use your brain
It's the only way to change our pain
Get educated on whatever you want to learn to do
It will benefit others as well as you
Pay attention to your reality
And help stop police brutality

Thank You

It was good being with you everyday
Doing everything together
From work to play
It hurts so much now that you're gone
And now I feel so alone
I miss you so much
That I'm trying to relive your touch
It's impossible because no one compares to you
You were the best love I ever knew
I believe you were the one for me
My eyes are watering so much
That it's so hard to see
Will I ever get you back?
Is all I think
So stressed, I just want to drink
Life goes on down the road
And offers a buffet of more
I will remember you no matter what
Thank you for your deep love and soft touch

My Unborn Child

My unborn child
I'm sorry it's been a while
I never heard one sound
I should have done more to bring you around
I would have love you boy or girl
You would have been my first and my world
I think about you everyday
There's so much I wish I could change
I blame myself more than your mother
It's crazy because neither one of us can have another
Even if we're able to
We'll always remember you
It drives me crazy daily
I didn't even try to keep you baby
I let your mother decide what she wanted
I thought it was relief but I'm actually haunted
It was my fault for using a dream
For her to make you into something unseen
You would be here, if I played a bigger part
My unborn child; I'm sorry with all my heart

Mom

You brought me here
And gave me life
Doing your best
To teach me wrong from right
You did well but I made my own choices
Some out of anger and some out of intellect
I don't know what altered
My heart, mind and soul
But it kept me from being whole
I love you Mom
And always will
But this is how I feel
Even though we weren't and aren't that close
I still love you the most
I think that you're the best mother
And I wouldn't trade you for another
I don't know where I got lost
But it wasn't because of you
I want to love and wish no one harm
This is the greatest thing you taught me; Mom

Momma

Momma, you're the best person I've ever known
I'll never experience again the love you've shown
Alone, raising five boys and one girl
I believe that you're the strongest person in the world
You're so intelligent with room to grow
Some people will never acquire the knowledge you know
You worked hard and stayed in church
Kept your composure in times of hurt
I love you unconditionally
It's not because it's something traditionally
Some would have gave up on my sister, brothers and I
Enjoy your peaches for the rest of your days
I hope God answers the majority of the prayers you pray
Thank you for always being true to yourself
It's rare in people and an overlooked wealth
I love you momma with all my heart
It's unmeasurable on any chart
I know all six of us brought you drama
I'm glad at the end of the day that you're our momma
I apologize for every single thing
I was only being a human being

Senses

I smell something loud, sweet and fresh
Is roaring loud making a wet mess
I hear a buzz and multiple tunes
It's an unknown musical under the moon
I taste something sweet but also sour
It's soft and edible at any hour
I feel something so warm and soft
It's something to sleep with and can't be bought
I see something colorful with the perfect shape
It's something beautiful and considered great
We take it for granted with lack of attention
Take some time out and enjoy your senses
I can smell different aromas with my nose
I can feel the warm massage on my toes
I can see what a dim or bright light
I can taste every flavor with one bite
I can hear everything all around
It's beautiful to close your eyes and focus on sound
If anything becomes too dense
Overcome it by using your sense

Sex

Sex is good and extremely physical
It's better when you focus on the mental
Sex can be fast or slow
No matter what go with the flow
Explore the body from head to toe
Enjoy yourself and put on a show
Sex can be loud or quiet
Whatever it is don't fight it
Let yourself go and be in the moment
Embrace the moaning and groaning
Sex is also an exercise
Something good for all lives
No matter what, sex will always sell
It also has a distinctive smell
Sex is beautiful and pleasing
It's relaxing and good any season
Even if you had the worst or best
Everybody needs some sex

Old Man

The old man is gone away
I recollect being with him during the day
Going to sweep up hair at the barbershop
Watching him paint as I sip on a ice cold soda he bought
I remember him always on a hustle
He loved his family with every muscle
Always asking his grandchildren for sugar
Which were kisses on the cheek
Something these days you rarely see
I miss this old kind man
And hope to see his face again
Instead of Grandpa we called him Gimpa
He was the calmest man I saw
He's been gone for a while
But remains in my heart and mind
Every day I take my time
And hope to see a sign
Some things we'll never understand
But I know, I love the old man

Memories

Memories are made with moments
And some are luckily chosen
I remember my first bike
A blue Huffy and the tires white
I remember my first birthday cake
Covered with the California Raisins
That I slowly ate
I remember my first sex partner Felicia
A sexy and beautiful creature
I remember the first woman I got pregnant
Our relationship will never be stagnant
I remember the first time I went to jail
It's the worst place I've ever smelled
Memories are beautiful and should be cherished
Sometimes these moments can be the rarest
Alzheimer's isn't a mystery
Take care of yourself
Enjoy and create memories

Talk With The Dead

I wish I could talk with the dead
So they could tell me what's ahead
Tell me what I'm doing wrong
So my life could be happy and long
Tell me how it felt to die
Answer my questions
To keep me from wondering why
Where do you go
Or do you wander around
Is it heaven or hell
Or do you rest truly underground
I want to sit in the cemetery
On a dark night to see who comes
To fill this void
Of which my mind runs
Maybe I'm losing
Or have lost my head
For wishing that I could talk with the dead

Sun Dance

I love the way the sun dances on water
It appears as a golden road
Something that's in heaven we're told
There are many images around us
That are truly elegant
But it's you who makes things relevant
We see so much with our eyes
And that's where the beauty lies
Enjoy the views wherever you are
On a boat, building, plane, train or in a car
Life and the world is full of wonderful looking things
Find whatever it is that makes your heart sing
Be amazed and ask how, what and why
It's never full and beauty is in the eyes

The Good Die Young

The good die young because I misguidance
Thinking that life is all about finance
Or hanging with their friends having fun
Getting drunk or high or playing with a gun
Why the good die young
Is not because of where they come from
If you think I'm wrong
Think of all the young that's died across the world
Now think of those who made it out of bad environments
Those that didn't is mainly because of defiance
Encourage the lazy to be diligent
There's nothing more gratifying than being resilient
This applies to everyone
No matter where you're from
Help keep the good from dying young

Picture Perfect

She is picture perfect
Someone who is truly worth it
Walking like none other
Seeing the jealous afar shudder
I love the smell of her perfume
Causing me to loom of us in the room
She's so confident
With a smooth, soft and sexy voice
It would be absurd to have another choice
I love her soft silky skin
So tempting, I'm already in sin
Her eyes are so seductive
I can't wait to be constructive
The kiss is so soft and wet
I had to slurp it
The feel of her warm, soft body
Felt so perfect

Confessions

From day one, I wondered about life
If it was wrong or right
I've learned and learned
But was still undecided
I was scared to be who and what
I wanted to be
I wanted to do what was right
But I didn't
Now my life is in the known
And unknown
I'm growing and becoming who I wanted
To be on the inside
But now I need to get outside
Stuck in a prison cell with just my thoughts
This is what choosing the wrong path of life brought
I've change and hope for the best
Even if I don't get out
I feel better since I confessed

Love

Love is something beautiful and great
Once you receive it, it's worth the wait
Love gives you the feeling of free
Something some people will never see
Love makes me feel like a happy child
It's unexplainable and extremely Wild
Love is sweet as candy
It can make a gloomy day dandy
Love is something all people look for
It's something that I adore
Love is warm and cozy
Nobody wants to be lonely
Love is what I live for
It's something that's hard to ignore
Love has an uncanny feel and sound
It's something I always want to be around
It's something that can take you above
As well as you take; please give love

Lost

I lost control of myself a long time ago
So long that I can't remember
I'm trying so hard to regain my strength
With everything going on I'm feeling tense
My mind is racing faster than anything I know
And it seems hard for me to grow
I search for a path or a light
Something to help me get back right
Smile daily, as if there's no problem
Knowing it is and wanting help solving them
I miss the taste of peace
It's so beautiful and peach cobbler sweet
I've wondered why: about so many things
It's been that way since I knew I could think
I want to let go but I can't
Because something inside of me is urging me on
One minute I'm calm the next unbalanced
Controlling everything about me is a challenge
Hopefully I got my point across
If not, I need help because I'm lost

This Place

This place is corrupt and always will be
It's not a place for you or me
This place holds the majority of my race
It's a flavor nobody wants to taste
This place is cold, dark and full of lies
Some people will stay here until they die
This place is loud, seldom quiet
Sometimes people are provoked to riot
This place is hard on your bones
It's throughout the world and well-known
This place can teach you so much
If you're not careful it can eat you up
This place is extremely lonely
They love to serve old bologna
This place is considered a hell
Even if you're here
You still have time to succeed or fail
Try to keep your friends and family safe
Encourage everyone to never experience this place
Stone and steel is all you face
Prison is what they call this place

Never Say Never

Whatever you do, do what you love
There's nothing else you should think of
Whatever you choose to do; be great
Don't have step or hesitate
Life has so much to offer you
It will be greater than you ever knew
Know what you have to do
And how to do it
A plan will make it easier
For you to get through it
Whatever you do
Have fun in life
If you love it
Then you know it's right
Whatever it is
You can make it to the top
Just work hard until you get there
And never stop
Like Justin Bieber, "Never Say Never"
Because in this life
You can do whatever

Beauty

Beauty is what you want it to be
It's not something you'll always see
Beauty is inside of you
It's whatever you deem to be true
Beauty is around you all of the time
Sometimes you have to open your mind
Beauty is more than a word
It's whatever you prefer
Beauty is more than a body or face
It's whatever you say
Beauty is your scars, fat and all
Whatever it is; love your flaws
Beauty is to be cherished
And kept forever
It's something that can make you better
Beauty is always there
Waiting to be found
Upon it, only you can place the crown
It's up to you
To make it your duty
To find someone or something
You believe is beauty

Rainy Days and Rainy Nights

Rainy days and rainy nights
I love them both with all my might
Candle lit dinners with good warm food
Nice, soft music to fulfill the mood
A crackling warm fireplace
To make you feel safe
The weather is so sensual
The smell, sight, feel and sound of it
Is so beautiful
The sound of thundering is so unique
My interest is always beyond its peak
After the rain comes the colorful rainbow
From the mysterious weather
There's so much to think and little we know
It could be a moment
Where things are going wrong or right
Just try to enjoy your rainy days and rainy nights

Be You

You are someone who is pretty in the face
With taste and a sexy, loving waist
You are someone with a beautiful mind
Extremely kind and hard to find
You are someone standing at the perfect height
Such a beautiful sight day or night
You are someone at the perfect weight
Believe me you will find your mate
You are someone with a distinctive voice
Guaranteed you'll be someone's choice
You are whatever you want to be
Do what you're good at and you'll see
You are someone with more power than you know
Only you can release it and let it show
You are someone special and great
The steps are there for you to take
You are someone with so much to do
No matter what; always be you

Believe

I believe in God
To some people that is odd
I believe everybody has a choice
You can be heard; if you use your voice
I believe, you can believe what you want
In the end I hope that you don't have an haunt
I believe in me and in you
Whatever you want to do; you can do
I believe everybody has a purpose
So don't ever think or feel you're worthless
I believe, if you want to fully understand all
That you knew
You're going to have to do to see it's true

Aspects

Life is a strong four-letter word
It can fly by fast as a bird
Life can be good or bad
It can make you happy or sad
Life is what you make it
Cherish it and make it sacred
Life is shorter than we think
If you sail wrong; your ship will sink
Life is all about choices
Take time to think and listen to your inner voices
Life is meant to influence and help others
Spend time with your sisters, brothers and mothers
Life is good when you're up
But when you're down it sucks
Life can be so many things
It's up to you what song your life sings
Life is better when you can love
It may be your ticket to get about
Before you're wrong or right
Think about every aspect of life

Hoop Dreams

My hoop dreams started from the bounce of the ball
Seeing shake and bake watching people fall
The squeak of sneakers on the wood
To concrete games in the hood
Incredible hops with thundering dunks
Comfortable fab five style long trunks
Long bomb three point jumpers
Driving to the rim with smooth runners
Watching Magic Johnson and Michael Jordan
Made me fascinated with passing and scoring
Made a team and learned the fundamentals
It's not fancy but extremely essential
My game elevated
But came to a halt
Because of a one-year contract
That I bought
I can only wonder
What could have been
All I know
Is that my hoop dreams came to an end

Street Dreams

Street Dreams came from being broke
Seeing the ballers riding gold 100 spokes
Old shoes and hand me down clothes
Seeing the ballers pull out big bank rolls
Wearing XJ-900 Payless sneaks
Seeing them with new Jordans on their feet
No money and can hardly eat
They're eating various snacks and slabs of meat
The music in their trunk bumping and beating
Leather or plush interior for the seating
Money comes and goes fast as hell
So does life
Ending up dead or in jail
Everything That Glitters isn't gold
They say, "the game is to be sold, not told"
But so many are telling, known as snitching
And stay in the game
Continuously pitching
The streets or game
Is not what it seems
The streets is more of a nightmare than dreams

Lonely

Being lonely is depressing
Meeting someone new is refreshing
Nobody to hold at night
Is one of my biggest frights
Nobody to talk to or do anything with
Is really stressing
I have to admit; so I'm confessing
But if I end up alone
I can handle it
Because I'm grown
I will find a hobby
And do it well
Marking my path
With a story to tell
I'm not going to be phony
Everyone wants love and happiness
Nobody wants to be lonely

Living To Die

Living to die is what we're all doing
If you think differently
Then it's yourself you're fooling
Every day is a step closer to death
So enjoy each moment and make it stretch
Live life happy and to the fullest
Because you can die from plenty of things
Besides a bullet
Living is beautiful and dying is a celebration
After that is intriguing to everybody's imagination
How many ways are there to live
How many ways are there to die
How many ways are you willing to try
Dying is sad and people cry
But in reality
We're all living to die

Old

Old news, old traditions
Some are afraid of new inventions
Some people stuck in their ways
And can't imagine making a change
The old loves to be routine and familiar
Anything new is extremely peculiar
Everything in this world will get old
Some things you have to cherish and hold
Old things and people are truly valuable
Money-wise and can help us be more rational
Old is of an age, mature and advanced in life
Something beautiful and usually right
The old can refresh your memory

We Want ...

We want our way
And everybody has something to say
We want the best
Sometimes it just leads to stress
We want to stay young
But we can only remember where we came from
We want happiness and peace
Will the violence ever cease
We want genuine love
Something we can never have enough of
We want a happy home
And to never ever be alone
We want to always have cover
Sometimes we should think about each other
Some people love to flaunt
Think of what you need; not we want

Choices

Everybody chooses from right and wrong
Either way, you can feel it in your bones
We are judged by what we say or do
Think before you act and speak
And always be true to you
Whatever you decide you will reap our suffer
Please make your life easier than rougher
Your life will go where you want
Try to not be someone who's vaunt
Choices impact us more than we know
Do your best to be happy and grow
What you choose now will decide your future
In the end wisdom will always nurture
Even if we hear voices
Your life depends upon your choices

Control

I'm lost and all alone
With no comfort but my favorite song
Sitting in the dark with my hurt
Thinking about how to get things to work
Frustrated and confused
Without anything, feeling misused
Wishing for a way out of this hole
Trying to get a grip but I'm losing control
Where's my help through this pain
Here we go with this again
Drowning in my sorrow day and night
It feels wrong but feels so right
I wanted to go
But I kind of don't
Why? I don't know
But what does this feeling want

Life

If I could have chased my dreams
It would have woke me up to valuable things
My life was over before high school
Because I abided by a one year rule
I gave up on life after my year
Which is why I ended up here
Sitting in prison because I didn't care
Now realizing there's more to life
Than being a ball player
I care now, but stuck with too much time
How early can I get out is always on my mind
I don't want anyone else to end up like me
There's more to life than dreams you see
Live for your family, working and helping others
Crime only leads to prison, dying and crying mothers
There's more than dreams to chase
So don't let your life become a waste

DANIEL SNELL

Decisions

They were young and having fun
Enjoying each other's company under the moon and sun
Doing anything to make each other happy
In love and respectable, something classy
Through all of the lovemaking and quality time
A baby came and blew their mind
Still in school not knowing what to do
Time to make a decision
This much is true
She had an abortion without his knowledge
Not wanting to ruin each other's life for college
Inside he was happy and sad
No baby but he wanted to be a dad
She could have died
But instead she can't have a child
And that hurts her now

Grow

I started off young and small
Unable to do much at all
Every day I became bigger and learned more
Learning value with every chore
Studying my peers and elders
Love and hard work became my shelter
Knowing the difference between right and wrong
Is something that will help me live long
Life is all about choices
So think
And listen to your inner voices
Save something for later
Through the hard times
You'll be greater
Apply the things you know
And always continue to grow

Signs

Signs can be heard or seen
To recognize, sometimes you have to be keen
Signs can be big or small
Sometimes short or tall
Signs are all around us everyday
They come in every way
Signs sometimes they save lives
Stay aware and open your eyes
Signs can be in the form of people
Encouraging others not to be feeble
Signs are often missed

Friend

A friend that's true it's hard to find
People will play games, lie and rob you blind
A friend will tell you the truth no matter what
They won't agree on everything just because
A friend is always willing to help
Smiling sociable and heartfelt
A friend is someone you like and trust
That person will not be found for most of us
To find a friend you must be friendly
Finding this person will be tricky
A friend is out there for you and me
Be yourself and open and you will see
A friend comes in all colors shapes and sizes
Some will come as surprises
A friend will laugh and cry
Comfort you and is there until you die
I hope everybody finds one before the end
We will all find one if we know how to be a friend

I Want You

The Sun is bright
And so are you
There's so much we should do
I love your flowing hair
So colorful and full of life
Can't wait for you to be my wife
Loving your angelic voice
Something so good to hear
I always want you near
Baby you're sexy
And you're the only one I want
This is true and not a front
We argue and fight
But I love you dearly with all of my heart
And hope and pray that we never part
You're essential, like water for the body
A man needs his lady
I want you forever as my baby

Problem

Like a problem you stay on my mind
Keeping you happy is like a detective
Searching for a criminal to find
Your smile is brighter than any sun or light
Like a bodybuilder to keep you
I would use you all of my might
I would kiss you everytime
Like it was the final moment of getting married
Like a newborn baby
You would be carried
I want to spend my life with you
Like a retirement account

You

When I think about you
It warms my body like the sun
You cause my heart to beat so fast
As if I just finished a hard run
When I see you
I'm excited as a child gets
For Christmas or birthdays
Like a permanent scar
I want you to stay
When I smell your sweet scent
It makes me hungry for you
In a special sense
The taste of your soft candy skin
Blows my mind
Like a volcano within
It's the best time of my life
When I'm with you
When we're together or apart
This and more
Is what I think about you

Daniel Snell

The One I Love

The one that I love
Is beautiful, smart and sweet
But sometimes I push and shove
Why? is what I ask myself
The only answer is
Because it's realer than anything
I've ever felt
I miss and love you
And wish that I could have you back
But the past is the past
So that is that
Thank you for the memories
Stained in my heart and mind
Every love song takes me back
To our time
I would say your name
But I prefer to dream of you
Just to keep it personal and new
I miss the sight of you
And wish and wish we could touch
Regardless of anything in the world
You're the one that I love
I love all that's wrong about you
And I also love all that's right
About you!

DANIEL SNELL

Pooh

Life is short but
I prefer to spend it with you
Because everybody dies
But I'd rather die happy
And for some reason
Only you make me feel happy
I love you like no one no other ever
And I'm glad it's you
I knew from the first moment
That I seen your face
That you have my heart forever
And getting to know who you were
Only deepen to spell
The similarities and how I feel
Makes it so strong for me
I would never choose a soul over you
No matter what, believe me baby it's true
I've dreamed of so many things
And so many moments
Believe me beautiful, I really want it
I let you go because of what I
Believed could happen
But now I don't care as long as
I you can handle what will happen
I will always care about what you do
Or go through
Because you're my Winnie the Pooh!
Honey!

DANIEL SNELL

Life

Life is really a gift
And I've realized it goes by quick
Life should be valued more than anything
It produces more than any farm could bring
Life is full of happiness and pain
Enjoy it all, through the sun and rain
Life is a precious jewel
Protecting the best thing you'll ever have should be your fuel
Life is loving
But also troubling
Inviting others to party with you inside your heart
Never choose wrong over right
Enjoy and live your life

Still

I'm thinking about the days when we would talk and laugh
I miss those good and beautiful days of our past
I pushed you away which is something I still regret
The love and chemistry we had is something I'll never forget
A true and deep love was on the brink for us
I believed that my ugly situation would be too much
I apologize for making a decision for you
I still imagine having you as my beautiful lady boo
I hope that you can forgive me for any pain I've caused
We're all human and we all have flaws
I still love you and always will
I still want you and still in love with you is what I feel

Layer 3

The Same

Two minds alike, more than you know
Thick in blood, but cold as snow
Heavy-hearted, minds weary and slow
Two different souls hiding so many blows
Time heals pain and open wounds they say
But you and I know that's not the way
A destructive path is all we know
I pray to God that light be shown
Through that path of disarray, I found
Someone who's just the same

Head Over Heels

I can't understand complicated women
Massively picking raging my adrenaline
How can I win her imprisoned heart
Letting her know in her life I want to part
It's so strange but I'm afraid to speak
When trying it made also weak
Why does she hold back her real true feelings
Knowing she's committed plenty of killings
My heart would break to know she has no interest
On finding love I will mark my finish
She'll never know if I don't say a word
So I listen to the beautiful songs from a bird
Intense encouragement to go speak my mind
And what I seek I should truly find
If I can't have her, then who will?
I want her to feel what I feel
In her presence I'd take a knee
Because with her I am head over heels

My Anchor

Down in grief all I see is pitch dark
I try and try to escape this pain towards my heart
You bring along the shining light
Fighting my pain away with all your might
My eyes are vaguely flooded with tears
Straining to get up from the pain of my fears
You come along to give me a clearer vision
You give me a broader reason to keep on living
Lost in love and I hope to be found
It felt as if someone was pushing me down
In love doors don't stay shut
Your helping hand reaches to help me up
My body feels sore and weak
With you my lonely heart can beat
With your touch I began to grow some strength
My heart pumps with beats for life to length
Your *comfortness* leads me to be brave
Saying we can serve each other as a trade
I want to be your all including love maker
In return of you being my anchor.

Imbalances

I am looking at a beautiful image
Dancing so elegantly I don't want it to finish
Hearing the voice sweeten my taste
Admiring the smooth beautiful face
I am looking at music
touching the spot that tucks her soul
Loving her body from the inner whole
Grabbing her heart and running to heaven
Knowing our imbalances will soon leaven

Doing What You Do

I have intense and deep thoughts about you
Which have so long been routed and true
Music places the settings of us dancing and roses
Flipping pictures in my mind of your sexiest poses
The sun reminds me of your beautiful smile
Love you for life it's my eternal vow
If I could have you I would be so rich
My broken heart and spirit would all be fixed
I'm so in love with your beautiful face
Your soft cushioned lips I want to taste
I think of you practically the whole time I'm awake
I see days and nights we spend and take
I feel I'm under crucial spell
Crawling to your love because at first sight I fell
Can you see the scene of you and me
Taking you to the place for a lovers are free
How can I tell you all that I feel for you
By you being so sexy and doing what you do

If You're Not Careful

If you're not careful love can be lost
Look closer and there should be no fault
Signs come and go, so they can be missed
The love you receive may be the one you wished
Honesty plays a major role so there's no escape
So, be the captain of your ship, the master of your fate
If you're not careful fairness will stop
At any time your love and time can be lost and dropped
Being faithful is not saying be a hundred percent
So there is forgiving when rules are bent not meant
Sometime carefulness can lead to the heart
Love can be found and also kept just be careful
Playing your part

If You Were My Girl

If you were my girl
I'd bathe you and wash your feet
So beautiful I'd watch you in your sleep
Make love to you in rains hardest pour
Take you to the softest and quietest shore
I'd make you breakfast in bed
The whole meal would be hand-fed
A whole day we'd play games in the park
I'd give you my whole loving heart
I'd take you to the place you've always dreamed
Life would be more than what it seemed

DANIEL SNELL

No Chance

I had no fun growing up as a child should
Trying to do all the things the older people could
I didn't know the meaning of life
Doing as I pleased overlooking my strife
The lacking has brought a life-and-death situation
Things has gotten hard with lack of concentration
Living without love is hard to do
Something I didn't believe but found out to be true
Seeing things that I wish I could be
Knowing that it had to start within me
Not knowing where to start made my bed
Seeing visions daily of me being dead
Waking in the morning nearly urinating from dreams
Talking loud because in my head I'm hearing screams
Walking a road alone is what I'm doing
Heading to death is what I'm pursuing
Over my life I'm taking a glance
Realizing now I have had no chance
Wishing on the stars and moon I could dance
Seeing that I have no chance

DANIEL SNELL

Hard Hearts

I never experienced tears of joy
Usually treating life as a play toy
Maybe if I could turn back the hands of time
I would read every caution sign
The few times I cried was cause of pain
But it's myself whom to blame
At funeral tears never fell
Feeling only like a maniac to raise hell
Common Sense seems to be overlooked
But I feel my life would have already been took
Being secretive to all in contact
Like a boomerang it came right back
Couldn't express my feelings to those I said I loved
Those who loved or wanted to love me I shoved
But I want to change and sit like a dove
Wanting to be loved now pulling you close to me
What was I thinking of, maybe the feeling of your embrace
You being a part of us is what I want to taste
Hopefully you will find room for me in your Saving Grace

Difference

I once was someone who cared enough
As time went on things eventually got tough
I became worthless and lazy with no cares
Looking through windows getting cold stares
Being hard headed caused major drama
Hitting me hard and even my mama
No inspiration or sense of direction
Afraid to even look at my own reflection
Constantly wanting to punish myself and others
Not realizing the help coming from my brothers
Death wishing day in and day out
Overlooking what life is all about
Now a love fell hard into my heart
Encouraging me to move and get a start
Speaking words to me that are so true
So excited I don't know what to do
I try to be strong and live every moment as my last
Living only in today and not dwelling in the past
I try to express love and show a smile
Just being myself and adoring my style

Voices

Who is talking to me so strange
Going on and on but gives no name
Daring me to take a crucial chance
Supplying music to my ears so I can dance
Causing my heart to flood with fear
But then telling me to get in gear
Whispering ideas into my head
Telling me I am meant to be dead
"He's going to kill you", it says to me
"In a few minutes dead is what you'll be"
"Listen to what they are saying"
"In a ditch is where you'll be laying"
"Nobody loves or cares about you"
"You're worthless, choke yourself blue"
" Be paranoid that might do anything"
"Go ahead just tear up everything"
But this voice to have to control
Before it ends up destroying my soul
Having me listening closely to all the noises
A non-stop headache is what I get from these voices

DANIEL SNELL

No Longer

When I no longer hear it I will be a corpse
Body hard and erect as a stick d*** ready to bust
When I no longer hear it in my eyes will look to the heavens
I will stay as if gazing into the eyes of my bride
When I no longer hear it my temperature will drop
My blood will dry up and my love flow will stop
When I no longer hear it nothing else will grow
My body will be put in front of my family as if I was a show
When I no longer hear it my brain will have peace
The senseless death and hunger of mankind will cease
When I no longer hear it my heart will not pound
I will never be able to have my bride listen to my sounds
When I no longer hear it people will not enjoy my company
My body will be left standing and everybody will want to rid themselves of me
When I no longer here it my lips will not vibrate to love
My kisses will become a fading memory for my beauty
When I no longer hear it the opinions of people will exist no more
Constant inquiries about me will affect me know more
When I no longer hear it life as I know it will cease to exist

Voids

When I did it I didn't have time to think about it
I felt as if I was busting a nut and thunder trembled my body
The fire just kept on blain and there was no stopping it
To pull that steel gave more control than the president
The stones hit the wall and penetrated like rocks through paper
Rush in out of the wall as a volcano spitting out lava
The busting of egg shells couldn't have been easier
My psychological state was as it is writing this sentence
Dramatic doesn't even explain the situation I was in
Feelings of diving into a brick cubicle with no way out
Trapped in my own s*** there was no charm in to clean up
Piss flowing from my d*** is how light I felt
Stones all around my feet hindering my speed as if underwater
Bright lights yelling and pistols made me adhere to the commands
My silence is what has me vomiting and stirred sleep with nightmares
Life as I knew it had ended and became something I was not ready for
Paranoid, defensible and waiting any day to reap the seeds I've sown
Beating the government at their game leaving me a traumatic person
My time away is feeling like eternity when so much happens in the hood a day
Most will never feel the pain that we feel, or see that s*** that we see
We all have voids ours just get bigger until we die or get our lives taken

DANIEL SNELL

You

You take my life to teach a lesson
You snatch my life to give me punishment
You take my life for justice
You take my life for closure
You take my life to keep the streets safe
You take my life to rehabilitate me
You take my life to reduce crime
You take my life because I'm a menace
You only take my life because you're scared of what I am
You've only taught what will happen and crime keeps rising
You can't punish me if I feel no pain because of your walls and bars
You have no justice cause the system that created me is still running an creating
You have no closure cause you will always wonder why I'm evil
You have no safe street cause everybody's game for crime and my evil
You can't rehabilitate if I don't want to be helped
You will never reduce crime cause somebody will take my place
You will always have a menace cause we learn from you and each other
You take the lives of the machines you create and feed so often

Trill

My n**** you gone and the road to come back is closed
As big brother it's my duty to find you a detour
We was both hard heads stumbling on our own mistakes
Banging everyday to keep ends and respect
Little soldiers in a game bigger than any other ever heard of
Following the OG's even if it meant our life
W rose fast as a team cause our loyalty and we were real
Then fell so fast cause weak n***** infiltrated
Our team evaporated cause we had different views'
You wanted to be boss and top dawg
All I wanted was respect and longing for the day I reached OG status
I was tired in a game it takes a lifetime to learn
Big bro tried to live a double life and stay real
Times got hard and life got f***** up
Made another mistake but this time got caught
Everybody stayed trill and didn't turn state on they n****
No evidence with a reduced charge they sent a n**** to school
Never stopped being real cup a n**** on conditions
Found my way out now your boy diggin or his life
Can't evat chill cu I got responsibilities
Took too many oaths so my life is sworn to just being trill

History

Steel bars of emotional restraint
Time that flies and waits for no one
Bullets that fly and will hit anyone
Knives that penetrate whatever their masters have them too
Fist that knockout whoever is in the way
Weed that tears up brain cells
Cocaine that scrambles brain cells
Crack that fries brain cells
A government that f**** its citizens
N***** that beat the s*** out of women
Men who demand sex from women by any means necessary
Men who are attracted to men
Women who are attracted to women
Life that is faster than light
Diseases that are rampant as stray dogs
People who are dirty and passing dirt as if it's a donation
Evil that grows as the greenness of all grass
Loose tongues slicker than ice
The phrase nothing new under the sun means nothing
What becomes of a world we know will lose from history

Breeds

Cold Steel breeds burning bullets
Ghetto neighborhoods breed thug a** n*****
Corrupt laws breed corrupt politicians
Bad ideas breed bad choices
Disturbed children breed disturbed adults
Good training breeds good athletes
Well educated people breed well educated decisions
Fighting dogs breed fighting puppies
F****** breeds f***** up children
Sickness breeds viruses for all
Seeds breed crops for our feeding
Electricity breeds light for our are seeing
Trees breathe oxygen for breathing

Covenant

Lying here my mind constantly fleeing from my past
Beating me and smiling as it continues to beat my a**
Searching for my peace I pray for the winds in the east
Savage beast on my back when will this pain cease
On my knees continuing to pray from this chaos I want to be free
Bowing my head pleading for my forgiveness
Send me some help is my request to my Almighty
A Phenomenal Woman will be my gift and my curse
As I look up I rejoice my corpse didn't make time for a hearse
This woman in my life, our marriage I constantly thirst
The wrong I have done her to lose her would make me burst
My sweet serenity is what she will always be to me
Needing her eternally, I hope her love will never flee
Loving me more and more it stings as if she were bee
To lose her as my soul mate I'd rather drown in the sea
Let a thousand tentacles kill me if I harm her again
Crawling a thousand miles blind, crippled and crazy for her love
I swear a covenant between me and her forevermore

New Life

Birds I see flying with freedom
Wondering when will I enter my kingdom
Grasping and starting to reach for my dreams
No more walking through life with desperate screams
Knowing what I want is half my war
Waiting on the time my life will soar
Ending the days seeing my life wash up on the shore
To wed my beautiful bride is my life's score
Clouds drifting freely day by day
In a cell all I would have is day by day
Wind blowing old age in my skin
Gone are the days I live my life in sin
My blood pumping giving me more life
Now we will see how I handle strife
No longer will satan pierce my heart and soul
Giving my life to God will be more precious than gold
Not choosing death because I have new life
The Ultimate Gift in life is a new life

Make Me Crazy

Does it make me crazy I turned away from my God
Or am I just human for losing faith in the unknown
Does it make me crazy crawling through life with this pain
Could my help be all around me quietly keeping me sane
Does it make me crazy the people I've stood up against
Maybe I'm just weak because of the ones I didn't
Does it make me crazy getting beat by my life's lessons
Perhaps I am getting prepared for something greater to endure
Does it make me crazy rejecting love when she came to me
Or maybe I was scared to trust because the future I can't see
Does it make me crazy being blinded by her passion
Could it be that she's my life's passion
Does it make me crazy how I've cheated her so
Maybe I'm just human but not your average Joe
Does it make me crazy my thoughts of her with another
Perhaps I deserve it but two wrongs would make us distant lovers
Does it make me crazy I gave up lustful thinking
Or maybe her true love has finally captured my soul
Does it make me crazy I feel she doesn't want me anymore
Could this be our final chapter with love departs and we end

Reality

When I see her face she's the girl of my dreams
But now I feel it won't be all that it seems
She seems like the love that I been longing for
And now I feel this love I will fear no more
Her presence was like the sweetest taste I've ever tasted
I rejected her and now that love feels so far
This hurt I feel is turning my heart into tar
And I know I never showed her a sign
Not once did I give her a chance to climb
The way she appeared was like the sweetest crime
Gracefully she flies like beautiful butterflies
Wishing it was all about us as we search the skies
Building our own constellation every night together
Praying this one way road of love never sever
Touching her skin soft as a bird's feather
I wonder why was I blessed with such a beautiful creature
The girl of my dreams seems as if overnight she was my reality

Dissection

Am I slave of circumstance
Or did I keep missing my chance
International man of mystery
My own self my dreadful misery
Struggling and falling but taking a stance
Anger daily consuming my mind
Attitude so raw I'm bout to go blind
Life as my unanswered conquest
Desperately searching for my happiness
I got to find the key for it's locked in that chest
Praying constantly for the devil to rest
Begging for answers is this only a test
The ground slowly pushing me away
Cloudy skies getting closer to my weary eyes
Relationships shattering folding away my ties
Not wanting to be lonely pushing my insides to cry
Punishing my heart with the beat of disrespect
Where are we going in this life of ours
This is the thing that I'm trying to dissect

Fear

What is my greatest fear?
Meeting it will it bring me tears
Loneliness whispering through my trembling ears
I can feel it coming like a sudden rush of panic
Not being able to explain these spiteful antics
My life alone would be so frantic
Chancing the rest of my life on a love affair
Never knew my past could bring me such a scare
Stressing every day feels like I'm losing my hair
Being lonely throughout my life and constantly feeling bare
Forcing myself to become a new man
My legs trembling wondering can I stand
These feelings of rejection my God I'm sinking in sand!
My greatest fear I say my greatest fear I say!
Showering tears down my face without a trace
Lonely like footsteps in the sand without a print
Beautiful images in my face without a scent
How could I have sown such seeds?
All this work I've done are they all evil deeds?
My greatest fear I ask, My greatest fear I ask
What is my greatest fear?

Taste

Running from my own shadow throughout life
Keeping my back against the wall trying to avoid strife
Finding me and cursing me in every crevice
I still try and try to stay under the surface
Adversity staring me in my face and sour to the taste

The keys to our relationship is communication, honesty
and fidelity
If we do not have these, there we have no reality
Faking these things will only lead to our struggle
And eventually what we thought we had would crumble
I hope and pray for something beautiful and serene
Everyday would feel like a u unbelievable dream
Feeling like we would have each other forever
Doubting each other in any way would happen never
Happy to be with you and only you
Excited because every day with you feels brand new
Being around you daily would never get boring
And every day my love for you keeps on soaring
This may seem like an impossible task
Trust me,
This is something we can have

Layer 4

"2 Heads Is Better Than 1"

A head turns and a head burns
The flesh yearns and the mind learns
With two heads there's four eyes
And with a double set
There's no missing sign
With two heads there's four ears
You can hear the ranges
From far to near
With two heads there's two mouths
Which you can taste
What you talk and hear about
Two heads can take you further than one
With two good heads
There's nothing that can't be done
That's why two heads are better than one

I Believe I Can Fly

Looking through my window I see birds sit and sing
In amazement watching them spread their wings
Their songs are sending me to this dreamy place
Tears of joy start riding my face
Through my ears I hear a beautiful song
That surf the air all day long
In certain things I strongly believe
And which includes the things I can achieve
In my mind I soar to touch the soft delicate clouds
Birds fly behind in multiple crowds
In my heart peace I have found
Loving the lift off to heaven as my feet leave the ground
If pain is in my heart I express a cry
Which is when I most believe I can fly?

Let's Be Real

Let's be real, nothing fake, taking it slow is the best way
Don't want to be caught up in some meaningless mess
I want you forever, if it is real there's ups and downs
But love is the seal
I've come to a conclusion that I just want you
Making you my joy in all that I do
No more games, just fulfilling commitment
My desire is you so finish the hint meant
I want all of you nothing more, nothing less
Making you happy my effort is at its best
Holding, touching, kissing and loving me is you and no one else
So let me know and show that I have you all to myself
Giving you all of my time makes me no mind
You are the light in my life that gives a shine
Just trust me like I trust you
Love can grow stronger to be pure and true
Don't hide, show me what you feel
Regardless of the matter; we've got to be real

You're My Anchor

Down in grief all I see is pitch dark
I try and try to escape this pain towards my heart
You bring along this shining light
Fighting my pain away with all your might
My eyes are vague and flooded with tears
Straining to get up from the pain of my fears
You come along to give me a clearer vision
You give me a brighter reason to keep on living
Lost in love and I hope to be found
It felt as if someone was pushing me down
In love doors don't stay shut
Your helping hand reaches to help me up
My body feels sore and weak
With you my lonely heart can catch beat
With your touch I began to grow some strength
My heart pumps with beats for life to length
Your comfort leads me to be brave
Saying we can serve each other as a trade
I want to be your all including love maker
In return of you being my anchor

The Life Sentence

Lives are worth more than rotting in a cell
Your life sentence doesn't have to be jail
Your sentence could be life with love
Being free with a simple push or shove
People get a life sentence to a variety of things
Sentence to kids, jobs, jail, love and soul rings
There are varieties of sentences which arouses
Happy or sad dances
So the meaning is there are limited chances
Being cautious can spring repentance
Which will determine a good or bad sentence?
The choice is yours but it's framed in time
All there's left to do is make up your mind
Use all of your senses and follow the light
Pick your trusted and hold it tight
The sentence you pick is on your hand and time
The life sentence you choose will in due time
Arrive and shine

Crying Nights

I'm shivering because the night is long and cold
Extremely upset because I need someone to hold
I need you to be here right by my side
This shattered heart needs a loving guide
Wanting to stand in the rain to hide these tears
Wanting you to hold me and push away my fears
Hurting, I want to be the man when we begin
I'm willing to do whatever it takes for you to understand
My dark crying nights will one day soon be bright
When you are back in my arms wrapped so tight
It seems nobody is around when I am down
So I might as well go somewhere I can't be found
The night is lonely, quiet and pitch dark
Hearing and watching the winds and rains stabs my heart
Wishing you would just burst the closed-door
Saying you'll love me forever more
Eyes closed, tears streaming, feeling and knowing this is not right
Opening my eyes
I see you your face behind this crying night

If You're Not Careful

If you're not careful love can be lost
Look closer and there should be no fault
Signs come and go, so they can be missed
The love you received may be the one you wished
Honesty plays a major role so there's no escape
So be the captain of your ship the master of your fate
If you're not careful fairness will stop
At any time your love and time can be lost and dropped
Being faithful is not saying be a hundred percent
So there is forgiving when rules are bent not meant
Sometimes carefulness can lead to the heart
Love can be found and also kept
Just be careful playing your part

If You Were My Girl

If you were my girl
I'd bathe you and wash your feet
So beautiful I'd watch you in your sleep
Make love to you in the rains hardest pour
Take you to the softest and quietest shore
I'd make you breakfast in bed
The whole meal would be hand-fed
A whole day we'd play games in the park
I'd give you my whole loving heart
I'd take you to the place you've always dreamed
Life would be more than what it seems

Time

Time of quality is only spent with your heart
But there's also the times when you are spread apart
Time away seems as times stuck behind bars
So lay out at night play soft touch music and count the stars
Time is important so use a good and wise
Then there are special times when you're surprised
Time can be harmed and can also be charmed
Sometimes in the dark you are alone
Then comes your rumbling storm is stormed
The hands of the clock are meant for you
Time is on your side and it's extremely true

DANIEL SNELL

The Greatest Love

The greatest love to me stays around
In my ear it whispers the sweetest sound
This love helps me through my darkest day
To show me my brightest night is the way
All I can think about how good this love is
And in me this special love lives
This love accepts me with open arms
Love to me is rated as life's greatest charm
The greatest love shines its light upon my face
And the love I have fills any place
Love is the key to an open or closed heart
Which helps to establish a constitutional start
Love is open and my guard is down
It gives my heart a beat that pounds
To someone special I want them to see
This love I yearn for and wish to be free
I want to catch all the falls from up above
I'll know when I have found the greatest love

Scared of Trust

I have been alone for quite some time
So to pierce this heart would be the perfect crime
Together sharing this lovely life
Cautious she might hold in feeling as sharp as a knife
The risk I'm thinking to take of giving my all and all
So shaken up I might get hurt and my wall will fall
What can I do to bypass this fear?
When love is knocking I try to have an open ear
To hand over my heart and soul would be so petrifying
If hurt at all, inside I'll go dying
I try to compromise and comply to loves demand
Not being courageous leaves me in no man's land
I guess now I can go out to stand on the front line
For the mate of my soul to come and share what's mine
Scared to trust is holding back from someone
When it is said that time waits for no one
I just want to know if someone wants love instead of lust
That's my reason of being scared to trust

Can I know Yo Name

Ay girl can I know yo' name?
Your silhouette smile and precious eyes
Yo' momma's to blame
I see a glow of music and your voice
Chaining me down
And in love with you I have no choice
When I see you my heart stutters beats
Your touch of vibrant streams like music waves
Blazes the heat
Baby I want to get to know you and give my love
Don't be afraid it might be meant
More than we've ever dreamed of
Your angelic face makes me mmmm.... girl you know
My rivers wave and flow
And the top of my pop blows and rolls
If you gotta man I understand you cup
What this is, is real I aim to fill you up
My eyes are on you girl there's no shame
If you make me chase I will
But all I want is yo' name

It's You

Baby your voice is constant music in my ear
Imaginations of lovemaking through my tears
I ask you to look at me and say what you see
Me offering pleasure with an opening of washing your feet
I understand love pours like a thunderstorm with a tornado watch
Only if hearts are open expecting filled slots
Now I can see us laying down counting the stars
You can't be nobody's but mine
Without your answer baby I'm prying bars
This cell won't hold me for life I quote
So say it's real
No doubt this love boat will float
Baby I want to rock you to sleep
Provide warmth for you my lady
And love that is steep
The way I feel is really true
I just want you to know, it's you

Alone

This cold night allows me no warm feelings
Shattered inside I stare at my bare ceiling
Wondering will I ever become free
Not understanding what people see in me that I can't see
The corner in my room becomes my enemy and friend
The continuous thoughts in my head are unable to blend
Seeing others love and enjoy one another
Feeling cold and naked in need of cover
The rainy nights levels my pain and depression
Confused and frustrated is causing my aggression
I'm yearning and longing to be loved and to love
To me it's so complicated so I wear a thug's mug
So far from earth I can't feel a thing
What everything is to me it doesn't seem
It's to the point my heart doesn't beat and there's no air to breathe
I'm shackled in this place where there's no possibility to leave
I hate the reflection I see which is real but doesn't seem
There's nothing I understand but death's means and gleam
I'm a mistake and I need to correct the wrong
Because I just can't stand being alone

For You

I feel intimate passion in your expressing words
Over all your beauty I sit an observe
Feeling the warmth and every hug and kiss
You're like a wish I didn't miss
Electricity is around you everyday
Amazed at you I don't know what to say
I could feed you the moon as see my dreams
Out of all your body parts glorious beams
Together we can swim in the sky
With elegant wings high we can fly
Your touch gives me chills and cures my soul
I'm drunken in spirit and have no control
When you speak it's like music to my ears
A moment of face-to-face contact bring me tears
When we're intimate we become as one
And it seems as if nothing is undone
Bounce with you on the softest clouds
Would tell you I love you in front of the largest crowd
You are there all the time I'm in need
That's why for you I'd bleed

Is Love Truly Real

Is love truly real?
Please help me understand
That people say love will never end
Tell me when at first did it start
Beginning to flow through the purest heart
Is love truly real?
I see people claiming to have found the one
But all I see is a continuous run
People say they make love when it's really sex
When within the soul and spirit it manifests
Is love truly real?
People act crazy bouncing off of walls
Not knowing what love really calls
I want to know can you show that love is truly real?

My Deepest Thoughts

Sitting and wondering how to be free
The answer I'm seeing is inside of me
Knowing there's a treasure of pleasure
Taking my time narrowing the measure
Time's passing before my eyes so fast
I'm unable to meet who I was in the past
My thoughts are starting to bubble and double
Muscles in my head are starting to struggle
I'm running through a jungle with tears for years
Watching my peers here quickly disappear
I'm falling from the sky dying and crying
Revealing why I'm trying and whining
Hitting the ground realizing the suns shining
Understanding we're all living so blindly
Wondering looking at my deepest thoughts
Why did I choose not to be influenced by what was taught
Running and scheming staying in the shadows I always fought
Beatings and making sure the kids felt like s*** dad always brought
Moon turning so black it won't reflect off yaw silver spoons
Sky no longer moving stuck in its own trance while we keep sinning
Mountain tops collapsing humanity got everyone looking so strange to me
Earth we use to call solid sucking our black souls to the core
Fighting for nothing, living aimlessly, dying lonely these are my deepest thoughts

DANIEL SNELL

That Girl

I feel the warmth of the sun on my back
Lying down in the comfort of a rose pedal stack
I see a woman walking cautiously close
Her image is my sexual host
But I want to tumble around through her mind
See all of the beautiful things I can find
The sky is turning to the color of love
It's raining hearts from up above
How can I tell her what I feel?
In her presence my thoughts and heart she steals
If there's a chance of touching her face
I could feel the showering grace
She speaks with musical tunes
She's a queen of fifty thousand moons
Can I inject a memory of a life time?
So if I'm passed she'll know the crime
If there's any way of understanding the truth
You will never know unless you're you
It might sound strange at first hand
At one point in life you'll understand

Where Can I Find True Love?

Where can I find true love in all this drama?
Someone to love and hold besides my mama
Romance the old fashioned way cannot be found
All I see is thugs and hoes who come around and go around
I want something untouched someone who's pure
Who can bring me the old fashioned way of love's cure?
I know the beauty and essence of love and romance
My inner man I let out and try to enhance
True love for me seems to be lost
To have it back I would pay at any cost
Each time I invite love it crumbles and dies
Just wish I could find someone who ties
Love is blind by the darkest night alone
It is as solid as a rock or a stone
I'll never be the one to let love down
Real pure love in me can surely be found
I'll never fall if push comes to shove
All I want to know is where can I find true love?

Move

Look here my little sweetie
No games to be played by me
I just need you to reach out
Can't you see I'm in need of love attention?
Eyes exploring and my thoughts pouring
Not to be mentioned unless I'm in your detention
My demand for you is pushing me hard
I'm running in circles over you
Wanting nature to take its toll
This love for you is getting large
Can I express this to you?
I want all of you for life
Not for a relaxation for my d***
Love is understandable but not really
We will argue and we will be happy
If we just make that move

Dreams

I understand I can't buy you material riches
But with a heart offered with love
I know you want the best
But if this is pure then we are blessed
I can see you want someone to care for you
But are you ready for love that is true
I don't care what anyone thinks of me
Just to have you would be great
What I say comes from the roots of my tree
A journey for you through my mind
Would help you see there's nothing to hide
I constantly hear your sweet voice
You are a beautiful flower of lover's choice
I want you to be my precious queen
You know I love and adore you
Soon baby we'll live our dreams

Inferno

Walking alone through this place called earth
I wonder I'm not already in my hearse
Taking bigger steps waiting for my path to end
How can God accept me with all my sin?
Time flies they say when you're having fun
Why I had so many relations with that dumb*** gun?
Glaring through the sky seeing my whole life flash
All this pain I'm going through why I ain't make that dash
My headlights blinking but not yet over on that hash
Life moving so fast for me I need to take my foot off the gas
People and their devilish looks making me feel like trash
Drowning in hopelessness my physical forms fear me
The things I could do to you just turn and flee
Pain everyday fazing me like a sting from a bee
My heart still locked up I wonder who has the key
Ripping every hair from your wretched body
Hating every moment of your forgotten soul
Know more emotion will you show I took from you
Standing there crying now you wish you'd stayed in school
Thinking I'm just gonna let you go away you must be a fool
This new life is eternal so be prepared for this Fahrenheit inferno

Crumbs

I will beat you and flee from your boxes
Constantly trying to trick me, scheming like foxes
Releasing myself from your terrible chains
Weighing me down as if you want me to drown
Marching through this desert these snakes can't be tamed
Dragging my soul from me would give you so much pain
Times have changed and still in life there is no change
The Big Bang Theory has nothing on my ultimate bang
You can't hold me any longer my pain has brought me hunger
It's so much pressure when you've gone deep down under
No handle on my life no wonder it will end in a plunder
Escaping these ghosts only to be found again
Hiding in every crevice of the earth I can find
Daily I'm asking the Lord to send His son a sign
Gloomy day's dark lifetime I feel God has been kind
Knowing my condition I am the reason I can't change
Leaving my impression like white sheets I am the stain
King of the jungle every step is a bang of the drums
Opening up to me but sweeping you away like crumbs

Wondering

Are we at the beginning of the end right now?
Or do I see the same souls lost and don't know why
Why do we feel the dead can't talk?
Through horrified eyes and actions I see the other side
Victimless crimes got me wondering what makes the wind chime
Victims crying got me wondering what are they trying
My insides crying every day and every night
Skin dripping wet from all the pain I feel
Like spikes driving into me feeling hard as steel
How will we feel when our bodies expire?
What will we think when our minds retire
Will our hearts be filled with our deepest desire
Asking my generation do they appreciate being alive
Or is life just the adrenaline you feel from a sky dive
Often wondering what it will feel like to just die
Could I come back and spread my story to those who knew me
Listen to my conversations with angels and elders who died before me
Can our hunger be satisfied with knowing there's life after death?
Remaining in deep thought wondering if heavens a place like we thought
Will you be fools and put your trust in the men of the earth
Why can't you just trust the teachings of the Lamb that created earth
How many do you know who had such a celebrated death and birth
Wondering of men will one day leave your life in its curse

Layers of The Heart and Mind

It's you that have to deal with your life and death so stop wondering
And make your peace

Eyes

As I often sit and think back in time
Wondering if my life is just the same ole line
Is the love that I'm giving enough?
Or am I still just evil, black and rough
Pushing my all out into her is this really love
Can this thing be as beautiful as a flying dove
Struggling to know who this person really is
She's kind of like a sickness to me growing as a rotten list
Showering myself daily searching for this new man
Did I already die drowned by the fears of the sand
Traveling this earth blind, death and dumb
Am I Hector my life cut down like a crumb
My eyes gaze with blood filling my sight
Will my brain ever understand this struggling fight
But If I am me and me am I what difference does it make
Laying my life down for God my soul is his to take
Praying that the end is when I am ready
How can I ever be ready lest I pluck out my eyes?

Smile

Winds rage and road showing its might to all
You entered my life as a sand storm standing a thousand feet tall
Face that looked more precious than jewels
Smile so innocent made all my actions seem cruel

Begin

Are you gone away from me forever
This sickness I'm feeling giving me this high fever
Locked away from me crippling our humanity
When will the man in me stop this insanity?
Walking around this vast endless space
How many times must we fall and break our face
My tranquility hoping to be endless serenity
Life through these eyes ain't been no crystal stare
Every day seeming as my personal judgement day
Going through life with this blank endless stare
Crying out inside of me please who are you?
Scared of my own thoughts cynical mind set
A sea of red is what these eyes portray
But everyday living my own sad blues
Happiness, I think is my endless quest
Have I found it? Has it found me?
Oh I know I've found the best!
In this circle I know they'd detest
Look up on us as the rest and let's see who's just
Are you gone from me, locked away from me?
Let's be kids again let's go out and play
My childhood being my snatched from under me
When will they realize this journey
You are gone from me. Taken from me
Anytime I want to see you again
I reach in my soul and say let's begin

Demise

In the event of my demise
When my heart can beat no more
I wonder will I be measured by my size
When my blood no longer pumps
Was I ever considered a punk
When the last gasp of air leaves my body
What will those last words be?
In the event of my demise
Will my baby and momma lay me to rest
Is this life really a test
When my body shuts down and the music stops
Will the quarrels ever be reconciled with my pops
Those voices telling me which way to go
Can I hear that sweet trumpet one more time blow
My spirit finally becomes one with itself
Why will it take my demise for the love to show
Will I see my kids develop and grow
In the event of my demise
When my soul will yearn no more
How many souls left behind will be eternally sore
This scar on my heart will it be mended
Will the weight I carry be removed
Or is this my eternal burden
Will I know how Hector feels with his eternal burden
Wandering the afterlife blind, death and dumb
My mission in life what does it hold for me
When my struggles will be no more
By the end will I be rotten to the core
In the event of my demise
When my blood will pump no more
All the things in my life have I finally settled the score
After my eye takes its last blink
Will these eyeballs have an eternal sink

DANIEL SNELL

Demise Too

Life as I know it will be no more
Mama don't cry for me
Allow my body to drift off to sea
Remove my legs from under me
Light a fire pour me some tea
My flight out of here still won't be first class
To all the haters behind me yall still can't kiss my ass
For all the f***** that looked at me as trash
I won't wish my greatest wishes on you
Nor my greatest plots of demise on you
No don't die painfully with a diseased h***** d***
But yes die peacefully with angels by your side
Don't even try to suffer from Aids living dead and sick
Die with your loved ones close to you
Rather you not go alone corroding with maggots in your chests
In the event of my demise
I loved all those who loved humanity
Now I know it will take the man in me to conquer my insanity
All I did was for the smiles of others
So why all my life was I persecuted by others
When they talk of me in my death how will it be
Will they say I walked with giants
Or that I loved harder than it is to breathe in space
Maybe that I ran as swift as horses

Failure

Failure hits the soul like lightning through the sky
That horrible feeling that hits you and terribly makes you cry
Music to your ears when you succeed but fright to your heart
When you fail
Renowned and pompous you want to feel
But unbeknownst to you failure will be your final seal
Why have I struggled so is your question?
Hindsight will help you recall that you are a _____
Freely thinking and consistently failing
Striving to go forward but unfortunately wavering
Still failure sticks to the bones like honey

A Word from the Author

Ninon de Lenclos said,
"Love never dies of starvation, but of indigestion."

This is a true and valuable lesson.

Seldom seen and rarely given my heart felt confessions
Turns into some of the most beautiful blessings

It's better for me to wonder and have you always on my mind than to have you daily, talking and being around you all of the time.

I could be with you every day and grow tired of your presence, but if we have time apart, then my love for you increases in essence.

I don't want to lose you, so I hide sometimes.
This is when I want you more and my passion climbs.

Contact The

Butterfly Typeface Publishing

for all your

publishing & writing needs!

Iris M Williams
PO Box 56193
Little Rock AR 72215
501-681-0080

www.ingramcontent.com/pod-product-compliance
Lightning Source LLC
Chambersburg PA
CBHW061441040426
42450CB00007B/1162